Passing Stranger

POEMS BY

PAM GALLOWAY

Inanna poetry & fiction series

INANNA Publications and Education Inc.
Toronto, Canada

The publisher gratefully acknowledges the support of the Canada Council for the Arts and the Ontario Arts Council for its publishing program, and the financial assistance of the Government of Canada through the Canada Book Fund.

Front cover artwork: Shirley McDaniel, "Saffron Medidation," 2013, acrylic paint on canvas, 80cm x 130cm. Artist website: www.art-explorations.com

Cover design: Val Fullard

Library and Archives Canada Cataloguing in Publication

Galloway, Pam, 1953–, author
        Passing stranger : poems / by Pam Galloway.

(Inanna poetry and fiction series)
ISBN 978-1-77133-184-5 (pbk.)

        I. Title. II. Series: Inanna poetry and fiction series

PS8613.A4597P38 2014   C811'.6   C2014-905731-8

Printed and bound in Canada

Inanna Publications and Education Inc.
210 Founders College, York University
4700 Keele Street, Toronto, Ontario M3J 1P3 Canada
Telephone: (416) 736-5356   Fax (416) 736-5765
Email: inanna.publications@inanna.ca Website: www.inanna.ca

For Tom and Rose

Contents

Ways of Knowing

Moving Free

Epilogue

…if marriage is a kind of womb,
divorce is the being born again.

—Tony Hoagland

It is time to consider a cat,
the cultivation of African violets or flowering cactus.

—Jane Hirshfield

Prologue

Omen

The voice calls from the path
hums inside each small coin of new growth,
furled fern through dried leaves,
exhaled from shadows lit
by fleeting wings of moths, says,
tread gently over rusted bark
rotting back to earth, *step quietly*
to reach this —
pearl-white secret in the gloom —
single trillium.

Guardian Pine

Nights, I've shut out the dark,
real or imagined voices
filtering from beyond the window,
pulled a shawl around my need
for warmth, blanket
to my chin, grateful for latches,
locks and blinds.

This night, the blinds taken down,
the pine looms. Feathered-edged,
its silhouette presses toward the room,
black as the pupil of the watchful spirit
legend tells crouches in its branches
arms stretched over the living
and the dead.

I have listened to the chatter
of souls in the snap of seeds
breaking from cones in spring.
Now, winter's deep and silent well
has me submerged, I turn,
entreat that dark-eyed spirit
watch over me.

Labyrinth

the trail narrow
sword-fern and salal
hedgerows on each side
the steep path descends, soft
humus pulls my feet down

I glimpse
through trees
a flat sculpture
winding path of laid slabs
indigo slate and red-traced
granite, cradles
in rainforest's open-palm

step in
follow the path, step
by careful step
to my goal

heel soul heel soul
along the outer edge
the middle near
and again, gone
realization settles
there is no goal
no centre or end to reach
not the path
nor my every step

temptation rises
to break the peace of
concentric circles
yet the path pulls
to the centre
will take me there
will lead me out
the end in fact
the beginning.

A life

We looked more at each other
than at what lay ahead — the unexpected
curves. Etcetera.
I could show you a silent movie

but Rorschach does it better.
A pristine page and a black form
that re-shaped over and over.
At times, our life together
as an ink-blot was fancy-edged,
complex, a pattern with interpretations;
dense sections broken
by conversation and music
like the negative of a fine lace doily.

For years the shape had two parts
almost separate, each one
reached toward the edge as if for escape,
but a fine sliver, a thread,
a thin isthmus snaked between two bodies.
A touch, a word might have pulled them in
to settle again.

Then the darkness filled in
the picture, unbroken, solid, silent.
We lost each other
obliterated
in a dense and suffocating fog.

The bed we shared

Three days after the divorce is pronounced,
I slide over into your side of the bed.
I have kept my place constant
through these years we've been apart.
Creams, lotions, books and glasses
on my bedside table
the one on your side clear.

I sometimes stretch out my legs
seek the coolness of empty space
or gaze, early mornings, at pillows
undisturbed, recall
the way you would sit arms on thighs,
your head down as you summoned the will to rise.

The ghost of memory visits me less and less
my bed awaits each night, an invitation,
my books now piled on the other side.
I climb in beside them.

The Divorce Order

The numbers and the legalese
stand between understanding,
my full grasp.

As I hold the paper
and gaze at white space
between words, a single tear.

A tear like one drop
of rain
makes no flood
or storm

and I have longed
for freedom, sadness
surely not what I feel.

Yet, there must be
some reckoning
with memory, with love,
before this letter is filed away.

Time

Through the sea-side park, children yell
from slides and swings, parents on benches,
the way they've sat on guard for generations.
Fountains spout over bronzed and yellowed leaves
on the pond's surface.
Another autumn so soon after summer,
wasn't it just spring, winter?

I teeter on a log, grey and bare,
 a functional transformation.
Waves fling themselves over
pebbles on the beach as I brush
off my face strands of hair.

Later, I'll exchange money for groceries,
carry them home, place them on shelves —
the store of years. No regard for the sell-by date
all through the child care, the making of a home.
We were in it together.
We met long before time.

Transatlantic

This bed, in your absence,
vast as the ocean you are crossing,
black as the sky you hurtle through,
empty as the spread of canvas
before you brush light and line there.

I will let my head fall
toward your pillow as I imagine
you leaning against the cold
window of the plane,
each of us rubbing a cheek
against an edge, each
of us wishing for a warmer
place to cling to. The way
we held each other.

Stone

"Put a stone in your mouth."
                    —Advice from a Nisga'a elder

Feel it smooth, the weight upon my tongue
that wants to shift it this way or that.
Be silent. Let words trace
its shape the way veins
thread marble, light and dark.

Let love's honeyed whispers
smooth the surface
for the tongue to suck-swallow.

Let questions serrate the smooth edge,
a time-lapsed erosion, before
words of anger can carve
a gargoyle's dark protruding eyes and tongue,
fire in the throat
that wants out.

I will put a stone in my mouth.
Hold my peace.

Silver Night

Shaking out the bags of our lives
was easy then. Four suitcases we'd packed
with all that mattered, opened in a new place,
distant, foreign and desired.
The wave goodbye on a solemn, overcast day,
hands signalled an end, hearts pounded
a beginning.

Vancouver — lit, dazzling, busy.
Traffic driving a mirror image of home.
Streets shining wet, rain and more rain.
Mud slides on some highway beyond imagination.
Our glimpse of the mountains,
shoulders draped in shawls of cloud

Tonight, back in those streets. So much the same.
Tarmac glistens from days of rain.
Christmas lights in the hotel foyer,
on the roof tops, in the trees.
Bolder now, no more the nervous kids
scared of splendour. Now, we drink martini,
one becomes two, we break our budget the way we did
back then: one more night in a king-sized bed,
playing it royal.

Twenty-five years. A quarter, a portion,
a young moon, a slice — of pie, of life.

We walk to the harbour. The city's all grown up,
shows off its fancy clothes. Bijou cafés
open off a boardwalk skirting the ocean
that clings like black satin.

We advanced so surely at the start,
stepped stones across uncertain waters.
Now lights spin out reflections like threads,
warp and weft make an illusory path
so soon to swallow, submerge us.

Passing Stranger

Again

This sinuous shore —
every inlet around this coast laced
with swirls of sperm swilling
over herring roe on eel grass —
ocean turned to milk.

Brash and unencumbered spring.
No instruction manual.
Unlike our contained attempts
to pro-create, one safe egg
in a sheltered harbour.

Year after year, massed crustings of eggs
sway in the currents, careful mounds
waiting for sperm to rain from a swollen sea-sky,
while I wash and wash again
my own dark stain of loss.

Negative

(New Year's Eve)

One whiskey-drenched breath away
you come to tell me "it's okay."
It'll be okay, being a father,
despite your misgivings: no job, maybe it's too soon,
maybe you aren't ready but — okay
and you say, "I'm negative" and your slack mouth
grins. You hold me and stutter it again.
I know your tangled brain
has mixed your words and you meant to say
something different, maybe "neutral"
which did, at least, *mean* okay and if not
jubilant,
not ecstatic, that you are able
to accept fatherhood
and it will be okay.

Passing Stranger

Still not passed that fetus?
The nurse cajoles, jollying me along.
Should I have said *I'm sorry?*

I *am* sorry. Sorry I would never pass
a long, cooped-up winter listening
to the weight of your breath
through the dark, windows steamed
with the warmth of our closeness. In the night,
I might have passed my hands over you,
wondering that you were real,
separate but connected to me.
I am sorry I'd never watch you pass
a soccer ball down a field,
call out to receive a team-mate's pass
and end mud-spattered and tired,
in need of a bath and hot cocoa.
Sorry not to have the chance to pass you
on the street, a person I never met, catch your eye,
smile that uncertain, checking-you-out
kind of smile, a passing stranger's tentative exchange,
half recognize in your eyes,
maybe your walk, something of me,
once, long ago.

I am sorry I will eventually pass you,
a barely-formed collection of cells, coming apart,

disintegrating in the warm but caustic bath of my uterus,
so much blood and tissue, flowing warm against my skin.
I summon the passing bells to toll.

Quietus

1. Hold

Wheeled into darkness
light from the nurses station
hollows the corners of a bare room.

I grip the edges of the ice-smooth bed
feel myself slipping, try
to hold onto the child.

Muscles tense, draw hard
a circle around the belly
but still pain cuts through.

Crouched inside a shadow
and above, I watch the body move,
thrash its arms and legs, *No.*

2. Fall

Too much white.

I exist in bright clarity
exposed under sheets
cold and clean and the air
is falling, gathering weight
as it comes down
on my empty body,
forces out the cry I have held —

a shield
against the end of the mother and child story
I've told for weeks.

3. Exit

We have both left my body,
(that flattened form below, white-draped on a plinth)
I tried to stay longer, stiffened my limbs resisting
the tremors that shook me, as if by ending pain
you might also have stayed

but we both left

your exit messy, complete
mine: clean, sublime,
no one's even noticed I've gone.

Night cast

Eczema flowers, I scratch.
Skin petals flake and scatter.
Nights, I'm trapped inside my skin.

Shadows creep fingers across the walls,
move in. Barren Hecate's face
snarls curses at the window.

My mother is transfixed at the doorway
will not enter to sing away the dark,
smooth sheets to hold me safe.

Dead grandparents whisper there are stories
to tell, *come, listen*
their shades' long fingers beckon.

Invisible dot inside me
is the child trying to be born.
Small mark of grief at my centre.

Positive

Imagine a metamorphosis unfurling
from the soft-contoured sphere that shivered
at the start of its journey, pierced at its centre,
sudden spasms made two, made a thousand, made a child.

We did this: brought everything we've ever been,
ever done, down to a cellular mystery that forms itself
slowly in my body but shapes in my mind,
even in the first days, as my baby.

Doubt is a word I have never heard.

Wings

I glance in mirrors, shop windows as I pass,
watch my belly. Stroke it.
This is me but more.
Under my rib-cage, a small bird
is opening and closing its wings.

Unable to know the place
that is part of me and distant
as the slowly churning Sargasso Sea,
I awake when the kicking demands
my wide-eyed attention.
Music in a nightclub drums too loud
and the foot that rests inside my skin, takes up the beat,
forcing me out, on to the street.
I soothe and rub and, *pianissimo,* hum a lullaby.

Labour of love

Two weeks overdue and midnight heavy,
my belly must be weighted with rocks,
pulls me down, brings me to my knees
and still I don't believe I will have a child.

A backache that grinds inward
pushing my bones apart, and that heaviness
presses down, hard and long.
Why would I want this? Stop it, stop it — now —

but too late: I push him from me
then want him back; he's blue and battered,
soft, unmoving, his breath
in my breath, held.

Your blue body

Everything [I] know
          —Alice Walker

Robin's egg, cloudless sky,
one perfect sapphire
then you slip from me
and blue is something new.

Grey-blue skin translucent,
flaccid. How still you are.
The spot inside my belly
you pressed your heel into,
feels nothing.

No sound
but your silence is
the precipice I teeter on.

Less than a breath, a whimper
trembles out of the long night
of birth. You cry.

Blue eyes
hold us
through to morning.

Circles, turning

A summer past, a Neolithic site.
I centred and turned inside the space
marked by boulders.
Perpetuity solidified in those rocks shaped over centuries
by wind, rain and hands that stroked prayers,
arms that hugged their unyielding forms, bodies
that leaned into them pressing questions.

Beyond the stone circle the mountains
were stencilled against a turbid sky
they surrounded the rocks
as the rocks surrounded me.
I looked to the rise and stoop of their stark backs
and chanted their names: Blencathra,
Skiddaw, Craghill, Stybarrow Dodd,
entreating their gods for circles within circles
to protect, to hold living landscapes.

Hand on my belly I recalled the ticklish delight,
the butterfly tumble of wings
that once pulsed inside my womb,
the rhythms of breath and heartbeat
going down to the beginning of time.

The colours of fruit

1.

Nothing green where I grew up. No plants
anywhere. Grey pavement, red bricks,
oh, there — a dandelion's straggly stem
pushed out through a crack. Small,
yellow nub of bloom, tight
shut and soon trodden down.

Mum bought apples, oranges, bananas
from the greengrocer's. Red, orange,
yellow. Cheerful fruit,
firm in my hands.
Thick and sticky wax crayon,
I coloured them
in my book.

2.

We are mother and son,
picking blackberries, the bushes
hang low, the berries large
and soft, ready to ooze
at our slightest touch.

You grab at the fruit, want
the tart-edged sting of the juice

in your mouth, want to burst
the blackberry surprise,
eat every one and none for jam,
stick out your tongue at me — purple!

At home, you touch the bright lines,
scratches up my arms, want to know why
blackberries have thorns.
My fingers fold over yours, your hand
in mine, both of them stained.

Girl child

Every night and day.
I close my eyes, she is there.
Her back and the bob of her blonde hair
always turned away.

Here she is again: in the summer garden,
picking flowers, reaches for each one
gently, carefree and oblivious,
I watch through every season.

Spring, she's climbed into the cherry tree,
hides in its branches, its blossoms.
Winter, I see her shape in blue-shadowed
snowdrifts piled against the fence.

In autumn, she covers herself
with brown, brittle leaves, wisps
of her hair visible
through the rusted pile.

I watch her play in silence, wonder
about her voice. If only
I could hear her speak, maybe
this would make her real.

Desire

Is it biological
the desire for another

that begins much the same way
as the first desire for a child?

Like my clematis ranges
every spring across the fence

this thought begins
as an infinitesimal dot,

grows slowly but steadily
into an obsession.

I long for a daughter.

Ways of Knowing

The easy birth

Matryoshka dolls give birth
passively and painlessly.
Intervention is total,
manipulated open, emptied.

They soon stand whole again,
headscarves in place,
the perfectly circular blush
of their cheeks constant.

They hide the gouge inside.

Ways of knowing

1.

Alone on a deserted road, miles of dusty tarmac
stretched behind me, wide open fields all around me.
A voice calls my name and I turn,
open my arms to catch a huge bouquet.
Flower heads are full of summer:
scent of blooms, cut grass,
the sting of rain on dry ground.

I breathe in my new, heady reality.
My breasts tingle, nipples scratch
against my cotton shirt; four weeks pregnant
already I'm different,
walk with the knowledge of how I'm changed.
My arms are full of blooms as I walk on, head up
toward a destination
I'm not able to see yet.

2.

I drink too much water
squirm and wait.
Don't want anyone
to look inside me
but I want to know.

Cold slap of gel on my skin
slow sweep of metal disc across
my jellied-belly, ultrasound blasts
through me, if we could hear it,
loud as rumbling thunder.
Patterns are like weather radar on TV,
cloud covers the view then fine tracings
that might be an approaching storm.
Yet all seems calm.
I have no clues to interpret.
I feel nothing, hear nothing
and seeing doesn't help.

How to allow myself to think
I don't feel pregnant,
match my lack of symptoms
to the technician's words "too early,
abnormal development; no yolk sac."

3.

A silent video
names the parts of me:
uterus, ovary and this, this is fetus…
magic picture,

silence thickens, we could cradle it.
I'm sorry, so sorry
things have gone wrong.

So, now she knows too.

4.

Let's say
it was all a fantasy,
I'll let the idea go — but
then let me
out of this cage of waiting.

Four more days
another scan.

Four days

before they will tell me.

tell me it's over —
nothing growing.
Ten more days
before they will free me.
I am locked inside the death inside me.

Who would know

that a good and patient woman

might want to run
screaming, from herself?
But where to go?

5.

Being a patient requires patience.
I have succumbed to examinations,
my blood and my genes.
I have lain flat and still, held my breath,
proffered an arm for drawings of blood.

Now I am attentive and polite
to the one with knowledge;
his judgment, analysis and recommendations.
I must answer the question about what to do
immediately, because the doctor is busy.

Wait for "nature to take its course…"

there is a dead fetus inside me.
Not a baby, not a living thing
tissue poorly formed and of no purpose
it is lying inside me,
until it is gone I can only think
there is a dead fetus inside me

or "get rid of it, better to just do it, over and done with"…

Get rid of it.

The patient patient does not question the doctor.
But the questions remain,
hang open like a flap of skin on a gutted animal.

6.

No way to know
from the pink carpets,
soft-cushioned couches
and a view of the mountains,
that as he warmed the instruments,
smoothed his voice (but offered no anaesthetic)
soon over, get it over,
want rid of it,
my uterus would resist
as the corkscrew of muscles
spiralled deeper, turned
to serrated knives — the fetus dead,
now aborted —
beautiful day, he said, still time,
he said,
for tennis.

7.

My belly is soft to stroke.
My fingers find no shape
to trace, no curve swollen hard.
Fingertips sink into my skin
round, smooth, empty. I bleed.

At first, a comfort, anointing
the wound so carelessly cut,
so carefully hidden: uterus and cervix
distant planets in a universe
my mind cannot fathom.
I float.
Though I am walking, breathing
even talking, I am
far away.

Subdued. Surrounded by nature
putting out its best: blue skies
with weightless clouds reflecting
a still ocean, I feel nothing.
Until your anger flails at me to
"What's wrong
with you?"

Your words scrape me
again. Inside and out I am pared
down to a thin sliver. Flesh, bone,
blood. No tears.

8.

Is it grief
this wall between us?
This cold, dry silence
passionless
in its grip

that keeps my gaze inward
behind marble eyelids
while your eyes search for a place
to escape, a place
where you could lift your arms
to the sky and laugh from the belly.

The wasp and I

Trapped behind a Venetian blind,
the wasp believes freedom lies upward
beyond the window. Its goal:
bright sky and a pine tree beyond.

The wasp makes the ascent, fights through
a waterfall of condensation, diverts
to a zig-zag path across the glass, takes off,
brief sorties in the narrow air between glass
and metal slats. But up is where it wants to be.

Again and again it tries to break free
and then the inevitable fall,
close to the exit path.

But the wasp cannot see. Drawn to the window
and sunlight blazing hope, it will persist.
It will never learn
the glass will not dissolve or fall away
just because it wants it, just because
it beats its head against impossibility.

Lost

You were good at geography, maps
and reading the lay of the land, always
able to tell me which way north or south.

Again and again, a barren landscape.
I turn and turn, stare ahead
to find my direction.

Birth was a place you could get to,
your child coming to greet you,
a person whose shape you could hold.

The rest intangible, ethereal,
except where the land has broken apart,
throwing an avalanche of grief at my feet.

I'm expecting my sixth

for April, who could

Six times pregnant. Six deliveries.
Six times, the swelling, the shifting of internal organs
who knows: the constipation, the hemorrhoids,
the ripping apart, the annexation of the body
pummeled and kicked and the seeping,
weeping of fluids, salt, stains, and always blood.

Six times pregnant. Six deliveries.
Six times, all the filling with anticipation,
the shifting self, the slowing of breath,
the body opening to all it can be: life taking shape,
moulding around a promise, birth fluids
are warm to smell, touch, and milk drops like pearls.

Ectopic

Out of place and disintegrated
into a million pieces, scattering
into eternity like a supernova burnt out,
my anticipation of a birth.

I try to imagine
Fallopian tube:
black tunnel, microscopic shaft buried beneath
the surface, a secret: silent,
but wide enough to guide an egg,
wide enough to grow an embryo.

Not wide enough: a silent bursting and blood
seeps and swills like a slough
filling after a storm, blood like water
finds its place, flows to every cranny,
lies in wait.

No thought
beyond the gloves,
the greens, the masks,
the eyes. A hand
strokes. I pan
the room made ready.

Give myself over,
fall into oblivion.

I relinquish memory,
contemplation of what might have been.
Each moment resounds like a pulse,
a heartbeat trapped inside a vacuum.

Morphine is a cozy high, I am warm,
I am safe, I am smiling, I am safe,
I am alive, I am safe, I am not thinking
I am not pregnant.

Days later, home again, my bed cannot hold me
the way I need to be held. I am scared
I will fall from the edge:
no baby; my belly sliced and sewn
for no baby.
I weep for my mother to hold me, for a woman
who will *know*, to hold me. You tell me
you can hold me.
Do you know?

After reading an article on infertility and loss

Infertile: sticky, orange-tinged
water-logged mud

the earth resisting
seed. No beginning

no end, solidity
nothing happening.

Spring slapped down again
and again by sudden winter, denial

solid as a shimmering blue iceberg
pushing its certain path

through an unresisting ocean, hiding
the bulk of its blow down deep, down deep.

The grieving parents' group

Three couples and me.

We sit in a circle.
The woman opposite holds a photo.
Her son lived nine months inside her body,
died being born. He looked no more than new,
wrinkled, but far too blue.
Her eyes lock on his picture.
The next couple's child lived four hours.
His mother held him as he died.
My turn: what can I say?
I lost an idea, a desire.

Remembering. Autumn.

Let the leaves scatter the path,
pale lemon tears,
small stains
separate and precise.

Let them layer,
layer, wide-palmed,
rusted. Leaves
fallen from an empty sky
washed in grey
denial.

Leaves pile
against a tree, against
a fence,
deep as memory.

Deep as memory, against
a fence, against
a tree leaves pile.

Denial
washed in grey
fallen from an empty sky
rusted leaves
layer, wide-palmed
let them layer

separate and precise
small stains,
pale lemon tears

let the leaves scatter the path

Moving Free

Apple moon

When you cut an apple the moon's inside

All my life, I've seen a star
made to fall, drop its dark jewels
into earth to grow the story again.

Three years old, you show me the moon:
full, round and white,

the moon with flashing eyes.

By any other name

for Rose

Your idea, I recall,
dreamed up one night in a bar
and tired of thumbing name books,
I was glad to agree.

Now, her cheeks burn pink
with every slight breeze,
this name *is* our daughter.

But what of the doll her grandparents bought
five years before her birth? Kept it wrapped
waiting, waiting for one safe arrival.
Rosie: her name printed on the dress.

Or was it my mother's prayers to St. Therese
who listens, answers her petitioners,
reveals the image of a rose.

Arrival

Winter is subtraction, light and growth
pulled back, hidden, the way
I once dug down beneath black and shining leaves,
burrowed into clamming soil to bury myself.

My daughter arrives
from that place, her birth
a fast gasping fight
against the weight of earth.

We are born together,
my body in hers, her voice in mine.
Push down they tell me,
but she is coming up
pulling the light.

We emerge under tall trees,
the tops ring a brilliant sky.
We soar, mother and daughter,
we strip the stars.

Light against the darkness

(after a painting by Sylvia Wadsley)

this band of lace
once flounced and swirled
across a dance floor
supple hem of a cotton gown
or, flick from the wrist, a linen hanky
to wipe away a tear

painted here
along imagination's margins

darkness all around
the canvas border

it might be
the growing glow behind the eyes
between sleep and wakefulness

> *on-off in-out*
> half-dreams of what will not be seen

woodland surrounding meadow
shadows seep between
a lace of leaves

between is where I am,
squeezed

pull back through undergrowth,
ferns layer, the centre looms
more black, more black

yet, I will make a path —
forward-back approach-retreat

and there, through the shadow,
Aurora's promise in
a swath of light.

A rose, on the other side of the fence

Through fence slats, long narrow glimpses
of you in your sun-yellow dress
splashed blue with impossible flowers.
You flit by in stripes, snippets
of the story you are telling reach me
as you move closer then are gone.

Your image in pieces, the way it was
all those seasons of expectation and loss.

I stared through spaces,
summers and winters, seeing a daughter
who might one day play in this garden,
sing stories and hide behind a fence
where now, a single rose blooms
at the end of a determined stem. It's pushed
its way from the shady side, a knotted bud
feeling for the sun, now it's spread itself,
a soft-edged circle, outrageously pink.

Women's work

1. Little girls at play

They've mapped themselves a house
under the trees, now flick cedar branches,
and smooth the dusty earth.
 "Mother" is at the table
she's laid out pine cone cups arranged in neat settings.
Soon, she will gather in her daughters
who'll come back to her hearth, sip tea, chat
and then wash the dishes.

This is not the way
I imagine my daughter in the world.
I want to see her open the kitchen door
and run, slam it behind her,
no look back to check if dinner's done,
the laundry's dry, if everyone's home.

2. Sip Peace

This is the world:
homes abandoned, kitchens empty,
one pot left unstirred
after the family's fled — invasions, missiles
smartly search out targets, the ones that go astray,
the ones that don't —

women, children, the men too old for soldiering
drag toward a place where little girls, bellies fed,
might lay their heads.

My daughter plays house,
dreams goodness.
As I dream of a time
when women will tidy every room
clean of weapons, lay out honeyed cups
for angry men, who will gather
at the hearths of their homes, join the women
to sip peace, talk an end to war
and let the children play.

Pastoral for early summer days

Wind churns the field, tall grass astir,
a hand through unruly hair,
shifts, leans into buttercup, thistle,
cow parsley that flourish,
opportunistic across this open space.

An oak tree, centuries contained
in the twists of its trunk, has forked
again and again, tangled its canopy
in unfinished knots that cross our path.
One limb scoops down toward the ground,
You see a novel climbing frame,
 try a leap, stretch one arm
toward it. Almost. If only

you could grasp it you'd be up there
at the start of a climb, shinny along
that hefty limb to disappear inside
a pool of shimmering green, the leaves
like a shoal of fish around you.
You'd call out to me
like the monkey of legend who set free
the water and drowned the world.

You move on
where a fox has cut a meandering path
through the grass. You dive in

where the fox has been,
where its skunky smell lingers,
into its bed, its crouching-place
out of the wind. You lie down, roll
on the flattened grass, become a four-legged,
panting creature and imagine that, unseen, you'll wait
for the stirrings of rabbits and mice.

I turn as the wind's breath gusts across the grass,
across the flowers, lifts pollen in pale yellow swirls,
sheer as the veils of a phantom dancer
who retreats to the field's black edge.

Away from you (with you)

At the weekend cottage we find a note:
a chestnut in every corner deters spiders
and there they are, monstrous, legless decoys
that lurk to menace their live counterparts
as they venture from hidey-holes under boards or rugs.
Or is their repellant power a subtle scent, spider-poison,
swirling around each shining brown nut?

I walk unfamiliar rooms, look for spiders —
find none — imagine them small and frightened, in hiding.
Away from you this weekend,
I think of you curled around your worries
your hands, the way they fold into mine,
your long fingers light and silk-smooth,
ticklish as spiders' legs.

These days I see you, somehow, smaller
than when you bounced
on short, fat legs, eager
gasps between shrieks of joy.
Eleven years later, you measure and weigh
each experience, as you apportion meals,
only so much you can swallow. You hold
yourself
still, keep your arms and legs,
grown long, against your body,
slight, pale and fragile.
Your skin is stretched over the landscape
of small bones. They rise, sharp

under my hands as I rub your back
with lavender oil and ylang-ylang,

What more can I do than this anointing,
this smoothing of your fears?
I'll tell you to breathe sleep's perfume, breathe
long and deep, believe you can rest.
I'll leave you, calmed
settled, brush from my face
fine traces of silk.

Thirteen

Half a day
to listen to the wheels gorge the miles,
stare out the window —
the valley: fields frozen green,
irrigation rigs parked, stubbled land
waiting for the plough.
A rainbow scythes the sky.
Heading north, the road narrows, rocks on every side
like school-yard bullies: jagged-edged, solid
with unspoken threats, ready to poke your shoulder.
Through the canyon the bus slows
the road is slipping away as rain turns to snow.

      Before you left you told me you were going home
      to the place of frozen air where you were born,
      eager to wear heavy-lined boots, parka and mitts.
      Your new black toque pulled down hard
      over your ears, against your eyes
      framed your face.

Now your face reflects
from the darkened window as you peer
at a wall of trees, uniformly spaced
awaiting the chain-saw. No trees made for climbing,
no twisted or hollow trunks, not wide enough to hide behind.
But strong enough for snow:
white sculptures mound on branches, hold —

slip. An avalanche, a spray of winter
startling as a blast of wind.

> This is the story that grows
> as you travel, as I sit for hours
> stare out my window
> cottonwoods stand apart, their branches
> scrawl across a bare, grey page.

Photo essay – graduation night

1.

Here you are, son,
at the wheel of your father's MGB,
top off, a slow smile spreads
as I implore: be safe, take care,
as you gun the engine, turn
a tight circle and are gone.

2.

Ready for prom, the girls
are women now, pop divas all
in spangles and shiny gowns,
glittering on teetering shoes.
Along a bridge, nine of them
lean and laugh, shift inside
their long-legged poses,
want perfection but could just as soon
grab their skirts, leap the railing, run.

3.

The boys, who have the bulk
of men, seem unsure where to look
and, for just this moment, reprise
their grade six selves, happy

any place on earth than beside chattering girls.
Still, they're turned out slick: suits
and ties, pomaded curls, roses
pinned to lapels, they'll watch themselves
walk a broad-shouldered swagger
into the next scene.

4.

Your face lit by candles
is reflected in the table's
centre mirror. After the dinner,
the dancing, the promises,
the dreamy songs,
lights bright then dim,
you look down,
your lips form a silent O,
your eyes expectant.

Below us, only sky

Summer so hot
yellowed bushes pant.
Lawns spring like coconut matt.

Last night we sat out late, on the table
a flower-embroidered cloth, a bottle of wine,
the evening cool and quiet.

The clouds are moving different ways

and you pointed, left: lavender-grey
wisps scudding toward the centre and right:
a mirror image, moving inward.

Practised in the ways of the heavens,
the clouds slid smoothly
slipped into each others' bodies.

At the lake, we'd be sitting above those clouds.

How to place myself above the clouds —
easy in a jet, but sitting on a deck?
Feet firmly on the ground, I've always lived
inside my childhood pictures: green and blue borders
crayoned across bottom and top;
house, flowers and the people constant
where they stand.

But, I'm willing to go, drift
into your design above a lake
at five thousand feet, ride
a flat-bottomed cloud
as weighted as a smoothing iron,
look down into more
as they shift colour and shape,
lavender to lemon tinged with green
a slow-motion kaleidoscope,
no other world
below us, only sky.

This bed

First you built this bed
cut beech boards into slats
joined them together.

We wrote our love
like a pair of swallows
trails its sinuous story
on the air. Then the drama
of the swoop and the fall
as if the sky had
without warning
rent apart.

Now, stillness in this bed.
Can we enter the breath of silence
utter a bridge
one or both of us might cross?

Indigo sky

The painting is blue. Water,
striations of shade suggest movement,
a wind gathers the surface
unfolds it toward the lakeshore.

The background sky is brighter,
the sort of blue you expect
on an empty summer's day, a little fishing,
a picnic, a book for the afternoon.

But then, there's the shadow,
sullen indigo obliterates clouds,
pushes an ominous screen
over two-thirds of the view.

This scene was made by your hand.
You saw the shadow, the darkness
that pushed across the landscape.
the small patch of brilliant sky behind.

I see the rain that came. Thunder broke,
the lake surface roiled as the wind picked up.
Instead of retreat you stayed to finish it.
Your brush strokes steady and in control.

The end of the yucca

Ugly, you say.
Look at it, you say.
We stand, look at the yucca.
Almost twenty years in our home
It has grown sideways,
its fleshy stem has lolled
across the high railing
at the edge of the room. We look
at its trunk's jungle thickness,
its reach for the light, its burst of green
bright and healthy at its tip. Rid of it,
is what you want and we stand, silent.

This plant is as old as our first-born.
We've lit it up for Christmas, spiked it
with tacky plastic flowers, hung it with lei
gifts from Hare Krishnas long ago, all
to give it life. Perhaps, a life.

We do not look at each other.
You are the husband, you
know best. Aesthetics, colour:
you are the artist.
You swipe. One clean cut
and it's done. Chopped.

Now it's a foot of stem,

a few drooping leaves. You
let me keep it anyway.
It'll grow back, you say.

Laden

OE *hladen, hlaest — load*
1. *to lade — put cargo on board (ship)*
2. *loaded (with) painfully burdened sorrow*

When your Thanksgiving box is ready, tightly-packed
with olives and cheese, shortbread and oatcakes
to uphold the family tradition, gloves and a touque
for the proper Canadian winter they do in the east,
and not forgetting a stack of magazines, I call the courier.
"Do you have a bill of lading?" the phone voice asks.

I wait for the courier,
wonder, will he come by horse-drawn carriage,
the driver in black coat-tails and high collar,
the bill itself scribed in a spidery hand
that has scratched a quill
across a brittle, sepia-tinted page?

Does anyone still lade these days, when messages
wrap around the world in seconds, when no-one
sits, steaming cup in hand, pen resting
on parted lips that silently shape a thought
on the air before placing the words
roundly-formed and soundly black on the page?

Too many BBC period films in my head, the dock
where the carriage is bound

roils with travellers, loosely
interlocked like an animated puzzle, their movements
choreographed and rehearsed inside
a layered soundtrack, shouts of direction: this way
and that, and the crashes and rumbles from cargo-handlers
who drag and shift bales of cotton, lasts of wool
forlorn animals whimpering in miserable
crates.

And, look — there is one small box
destined for your small room.
We're long past those nights I'd stand by your bed,
check on the rise and fall of your blankets
as I drew the curtains against the dark
I never fully learned to trust.
I watch the box load, try on a smile,
as I think of you removing its bill of lading
before you open it up.

Ocean swimming

Mid-August, but the sun
has not yet warmed the ocean.
You shiver at the edge
say *no, too cold*
and *I can't,*

hold back, the way
you always have,
the world big, cold
too much to enter.

You want to tell me,
to explain how
you *just can't*
and I want to

pull you to me,
hold you here
against my warmth,

Then, the break
that is another small hand
reaching for yours,
gently pulls

Okay, she says
The water's okay,

Come on, it's fun,
one tug, you're in.

You scream
then splash, laugh.
the big-cold is
not so, you swim,

push and glide, slide
under ripples as light
glints off the surface,
off you
            moving free.

Epilogue

The grace of a morning's chores

This morning, a prayer
of contentment that I am here
when rain begins. Sudden,
pummel of the ground
gives up its music, its reduplicated rhythms,
pin-pointed beats drum in my head.
I am here, dry and folding laundry,
take a blouse, shoulders together,
smooth the collar flat.

I am here, dash out, move the garden chairs
already small pools at their centres
strewn with leaves and cottonwood down.
A small act of rescue, an offering,
to the gods of domesticity.
Look, I am here: pull the sheets
from another dirty bed, I am here:
listen on the phone, reassure, counsel
though in another life
I might, on a morning like this,
walk through woods
and raindrops.

The rain would
detonate in small bursts
as it came faster, freely soak the earth,
all that's green and me besides.

Aria

If I can't keep this technicolour morning,
peel the scene with one finger and thumb-pinch

top left to bottom right and place it
sticky-side down in my mind's album

then let me, at least, remember
the crackle and blaze of maples searing the air:

crescendo; let me open my mouth
swallow the golden-honey

candied floss of aspen and birch;
let me hold in my palm tufts of flowers

gone to feathered seeds.
Let me blow gently into the centre of them

release these harbingers of spring
into each day's misted portent of winter's arrival.

The same night

"…the same night whitening the same trees"
—Pablo Neruda

Memories of you emerge from night.
Sleep has left, fleet, through window
or cracks in the armour of my quiet body.
I lie, stare as if to the sky; as if I could break
from the silence of this bed; as if your voice
continued to lick my skin.

A full moon the night you turned away,
entered your new life. So many nights
since, the moon sings its luminescent song.
No longer silver light dripping

from finger tips across breasts,
but the same night
whitening the same trees.

There's always something…

between us,
between trees and clouds,
like wafts of pollen, yellow scarves
we don't notice until they dust
every surface, silent colouration
on the skin of our unknowing.

Always something
in the now. Attend
to scattered leaves, gold and scarlet
how they emboss earth.
Listen to the tick,
the drip of rain.

Something
in the way. Between here and there.
Between today and tomorrow. Like
the stretch of water from shore to distant island
and no boat. No way to cross the miles
of longing for the other place, imagined home.

Three echoes of love

When you lie back

after the loving is over

your skin

so near, our bodies

just glancing,

hearts slow

the merest space
between us

the whole sky
above us

the silencing rain

comes down

I lie beside you

reach out and touch

touch your skin

turned away, now

the loving is over

empty, the space

I look far away

I see it coming

the rain comes down

on our bodies.

Future

I wake, my body wrenched open,
my heart exposed.

Unpractised in the art of Saudade,
a numb sensibility keeps my arms

tight at my sides. I cannot fling
my soul into dark night, wait

for dawn to clear the sky, streaks
of lemon, gold, small glimpse —
hope on my horizon.

Now: the Artist's ex-wife

I followed

        you along forest paths

always loved our

        sensuous lines

body and mind

        the vaulted ceilings of cathedrals.

You are

        gone
        an empty space beside me

        one sweep

in anger

        a smooth canvas skin.

broken

once

        arms full of roses.

Learn to let go

(from a story of Zen traditional teaching)

At the edge of the ocean
waves roll in, lay down
an invitation at my feet.
Words form in the trickle of foam
lacing into the sand.
Step in. Come in.
I don't move.

Behind a low wall, a line of people
gaze at sunset's trail of liquid copper,
Each has clambered onto the top
for an unobstructed view of the sky,
and to absorb the light.
I wait.

I pause at the edge of a cliff
peer down at the water calm, clear blue.
Between the rocks below, a pod of killer whales
stitch a course. The ease and grace
of their sleek bodies a luminous chant.
Come with us.

       I could jump.
       I dreamt this fall

Arms open, air carries me
as acceleration and the wind's
metallic song streak my body,
the water waits to swallow me.

But, when I land, water is earth,
grass springs at my feet
and I stand.

I return

for Darlene

I return to this room, come back
to a conversation left on pause.
This room and its objects
reposit story: the spinning wheel in the corner;
on the walls: woven trees in a circle of wool;
a tapestry flower, bold and blowsy,
pistils and stamens declare its seed is scattered,
carried on the wind that has blown
through our lives.

Weekday mornings or afternoons,
we'd sit and talk. Kitchen conversations,
your copper teapot kept hot on the stove,
we re-filled our china mugs with rose-hip tea;
it steamed summer through long winters.
The babies slept while we shared recipes:
apple-blackberry muffins, squash soup.
And then, our fears of mushroom clouds
would we see our children grown?

More often, now, we talk by phone.
A thousand miles apart,
we seldom share a pot of tea.
But here we are, me curled
in the corner of your couch, you rocking
in the chair you nursed your babies in.

Now, we talk over wine and worries. More
than middle-aged, our husbands gone from our lives,
ideas for *what now* float between us. We wish,
again, to catch the seeds that fly,
plant them in newly tilled earth. Time still
to grow a garden.

On Galiano

I have seen arbutus
reaching up like dancers
painted red with the stain of silent ritual.

This tree stands
like a fork of lightning
grabbed by the earth,
it shouts of all that I could hold,
the entire sky,
if I would open up my arms, stretch
if I would let the air smooth my skin,
let it peel, know
there are stronger layers beneath.

I sit in rooms with women

Ideas flash as fast as the shreds
from the mandoline. Cabbage,
cucumber and carrot
fall with barely a touch, settle
into the centre of the wrap,
permit an enfolding
disturbed only by slow
bites and *mmm, delicious* —
must have the recipe.

And just as quick: a turn.
The book we're gathered to discuss
pulls the conversation
into the backstreets of the city,
into the life of another woman who tells
how crime was her route to a meal,
another who writes to feel whole.

Ours is the spirit
that knows what it wants
and is unashamedly Woman.
Beautiful and clever,
all-knowing and yes, wise.
We may one day steal to stay alive,
on another, realize
that living is multi-hued

and we manage all its shades and colours
the way we might throw
a black shawl, casual,
calculated, across a red cowl-neck sweater.

Hand in a 3-paned mirror – an early morning meditation

Too early to rise,
my eyes open to the mirror
and it's triptych of images.

Centre: my body under blue
covers, my hand hangs pale
like dove wings
feather-fingers swollen
roughened, after a long flight.
Still but not lifeless,
now and then imperceptible lift.

Left: blue on blue,
the rise of a shrouded landscape
something human suggested
maybe twilight darkened hills,
the cloud-worried sky
to traverse before day.

Right: reflects my hand
from an angle. Now,
the dove rests or is its
wing broken?
We fall into sleep, the dove and I
weary after our long journeys.

Now, in a dream,
the white dove coos,
my hand proffers a perch.

Acknowledgements

My sincere thanks to:

Fiona Lam who first suggested I should write about pregnancy and loss, birth and motherhood, topics of such importance in women's lives.

Heidi Greco who provided invaluable reading and editing of the manuscript.

Jean Mallinson, my constant friend and mentor for her attuned ear and attention to detail as she read many of these poems.

Women of the Compossibles poetry study group for the inspiration of their dedication to poetry.

Members of various writing groups I have belonged to where the seed of some of these poems was planted.

Darlene Westerman, my surrogate sister, for her listening and support.

Karen Drexel for the quiet of her beautiful Gulf Island home where, at times, I worked on the manuscript.

Gervais Fox who listens, reads and always has a new and intelligent perspective to offer.

The epigraph to "The same night" is from Pablo Neruda's "Tonight I can write the saddest lines."

The poem "Away from you (with you) won a high commendation award in the Petra Kenney Poetry Contest (UK).

"Now: the artist's ex-wife" is a found poem from my original, "The artist's wife," published in *Quintet: Themes & Variations,* a collaborative book by Jean Mallinson, Pam Galloway, Eileen Kernaghan, Clelie Rich and Sue Nevill (Ekstasis Editions, 1998).

The reference to marble eyelids in the long poem "Ways of Knowing" is from the poem "Grief" by Elizabeth Barret Browning.

Lastly, my love and thanks to my now grown children Tom and Rose for their continuing inspiration in my writing and in my life.

Photo: Patrik Jandak

Pam Galloway lives, works and writes in Vancouver and has an MFA in Creative Writing from the University of British Columbia. Her poetry and non-fiction have been featured on CBC radio and has been published in numerous Canadian literary magazines including *The Antigonish Review, The New Quarterly, Contemporary Verse 2, Grain, Descant, Dandelion, Event, The New Orphic Review, Room of One's Own* and twice on the website of the Canadian Parliamentary Poet Laureate. Her first collection of poetry, *Parallel Lines,* was published in 2006.